LEAP OF FAITH

LEAP OF FAITH

A 29 DAY CHALLENGE TO BE BETTER TOGETHER

TERRELL BATTTEN • LANCE GOOSLBY
DEFOREST MAPP • THADDEUS PARSONS
DWIGHT SHAWROD RIDDICK II
THOMASENA RANEE ROBINSON

LEAP OF FAITH
A 29 Day Challenge to Be Better Together

Copyright © 2020 by Terrell Batten, Lance Goolsby, Deforest Mapp, Thaddeus Parsons, Dwight Shawrod Riddick II, Thomasena Ranee Robinson
All rights reserved.

All rights reserved. This book is protected by the copyright laws of the United States of America. This book may not be copied or reprinted for commercial gain or profit. The use of quotations or occasional page copying for personal or group study is permitted and encouraged. Permission will be granted upon request.

Unless otherwise identified, Scripture quotations are from the New Living Translation. Copyright © 1996, 2004, 2015 by Tyndale House Foundation. Used by permission of Tyndale House Publishers, Inc., Carol Stream, Illinois 60188.
All rights reserved.

Final Step Publishing, LLC

PO Box 1441
Suffolk, VA 23439

For Worldwide Distribution. Printed in U.S.A.

Soft cover ISBN: 978-1-7342371-4-6

Dedicated To

Ella Mae Simons, the sister of Mary Brite who was born on a Leap Year and made her porch on Fentress Road in Chespeake, VA, a meeting place for a community to come together. May your legacy encourage others to stay connected to each other and most importantly stay connected to Jesus Christ.

Acknowledgements

We want to thank God for His love that allowed these authors to unite and through God synergy produce this leap year guide. Thank you to Worship Pastor Terrell Batten for the sacrifices he has made to join our church family. The spiritual tune of his textual homiletics created a great harmony among our writers. Thank you to Deacon Lance Goolsby who would give weekly time during work to make time to do this God work. His mind is as sharp as his name would suggest—he's a lance in God's hand—and he wields the sword of the spirit fiercely. His heart for God and love for God's people spill over into his biblical interpretation and blesses us all. We are thankful for Thaddeus Parsons and the depth of information that he has. Whenever he took a swing at interpreting scripture he would do so with the eye of a tiger and was always par for the course in speaking the whole truth. He is a true scholar, and it is evident that God has blessed his constant study with anointed revelation that not only inspires life transformation but forces spiritual growth. Big thanks to Deforest Mapp for the wealth of knowledge that he possesses and is willing to share. It is obvious that he is led by God. Like a cartographer he would help us find the hidden treasures buried beneath scripture and practical relevance. To Thomasena Renee Robinson, we owe a huge thanks. In following a calling from God, she organized our thoughts, deposited rare jewels of theological wisdom into each conversation, and with a godly radiance illuminated the scriptures in a way that helps others see Jesus. She has used her anointing to rob Satan of souls and present them back to Jesus as disciples. Lastly, but definitely not least, we thank God for Dr. Jennell Riddick for spending time in the presence of God and emerging with this time that God gave birth to the leap of faith during the leap year instructions, and from there she delivered it to our team and commissioned us to walk in it while giving life to a God-conceived assignment. I am thankful as a pastor and a brother of this anointed team of Christian educators to come alongside them and prepare a resource that I believe will launch a community into the direction of Jesus Christ while soaring on the wings of faith.

—Dr. Dwight Shawrod Riddick II
Senior Pastor St Mark Missionary Baptist Church
Portsmouth, VA

CONTENTS

Foreword	10
Preface	11
Day 1: Evangelize Day 1	16
Day 2: Pray for Our Community	18
Day 3: Pray for Our Country	20
Day 4: Pray for All Youth	22
Day 5: Read John 17	24
Day 6: Attend Bible Study	26
Day 7: Invite Someone to Church Part 1	28
Day 8: Invite Someone to Church Part 2	30
Day 9: Abstain from TV	32
Day 10: Abstain from Social Media	34
Day 11: A Well-being Call	36
Day 12: Reconcile an Estranged Relationship	38
Day 13: Make a Gratitude List	40
Day 14: Make or Buy a Gift	42
Day 15: Buy or Make Lunch for Someone	44

Day 16: Evangelize Day 2   46

Day 17: Give 3-5 Genuine Compliments   48

Day 18: Volunteer at a School   50

Day 19: Donate Used Goods to Goodwill   52

Day 20: 30-Minute Physical Activity   54

Day 21: Spend Time in a Garden or   56
         in Nature

Day 22: Study a Member of the   58
         "Hebrews Hall of Faith"

Day 23: Visit the Library   60

Day 24: Six Steps of Success   62

Day 25: Learn a New Vocabulary Word   64

Day 26: Write a Prayer   66

Day 27: Parking Lot Prayer   68

Day 28: In God We Trust   70

Day 29: Evangelize Day 3   72

FOREWORD

What is faith? According to Hebrews 12, "Faith is the substance of things hoped for, the evidence of things not seen." The Bible also tells us that without faith it is impossible to please God. So, what does that have to do with you? We all should desire to please God, therefore faith is essential. In addition to pleasing God, our faith helps us possess the promises of God. You can't move forward into the blessings of God without believing and trusting God. Most of us would admit that we desire what God has for us, however, are we willing to believe God and take a leap to possess what He has promised?

When the situation looks bleak, we must believe God. When the odds seem stacked against us, believe God. God doesn't have to work with odds, He has the final say and specializes in doing the unusual. Remember, God is able to do exceedingly abundantly above all that you can ask or think. The miracles and promises of God are not reserved for a few special people. His promises are for all who believe. He wants to do something incredible in your life. Believe God. Let your action match your expectation. If you can believe God for the great, take a leap with us!

—Dr Jennell Riddick

PREFACE

Did you see the image on the cover? That is a picture of a fearless man not just taking a leap but taking a leap back first heading into unseen waters. Do you think you could take a leap like that? Obviously, I do not mean into the water from off of a mountain. I mean could you try something new when the outcome is unknown. Could you do it with your head looking high to the God who takes care of you? I'm sure you're saying, "I know I should be able to, but I'm not sure." Do not be discouraged; this is the case for many of us. Having the ability to leap is drastically different than making the attempt.

Author Scott Aughtmon writes about the African Impala (a deer-looking antelope from Africa) that can jump 10 feet high and cover a distance of more than 30 feet. However, these animals have a strange characteristic. These high jumping creatures are often kept **in zoo enclosures behind a <u>3-foot wall</u>. Yes, you read that right. A 3-foot wall.** Trust me, your math is not off nor are you crazy. It is true for them that they can jump 10 feet up, but a 3-foot wall can stop them. I'm sure you are wondering how is that possible. They have almost 7 feet, that's 2 inches less than the height of NBA star Kevin Durant. They have clearly enough clearance to make the jump and be free. So why do they live trapped? It's unfortunately easy to explain while at the same time a great lesson for us all. These animals WILL NOT JUMP IF THEY CANNOT SEE where their feet will land. **That means that Impalas stay <u>trapped and living with limits</u>** because they refuse to go where they can't see themselves. Wow! Isn't that both a tragedy and a lesson. How many 3-foot fences have held us back, locked us is in, and caused us to live beneath our potential simply because we were fearful of leaping into a new area of life that we could not see ourselves in? No longer can this be. We must jump. We must be what God has called us to be, and go where He is beckoning us to go, even if we cannot see it. The leap does not just eradicate our fear, it is evidence of our faith. This is what we mean when we say, take a LEAP OF FAITH. Here are a few of my quotes on faith.

Award winning author of "*Chase the Lion*" Mark Batterson says, "Faith is climbing out on a limb, cutting it off, and watching the tree fall." For me this reminds me that often the leap of faith will leave you hanging out alone and floating in the unknown, but it is a place where God is sustaining you.

In his most famous "I Have a Dream" speech, Dr Martin Luther King Jr. once said, "Faith is taking the first step even when you can't see the whole staircase." Living in a two-story house for most of my life I always pictured this step as a step down. Not a step up. Going up stairs often provides you the ability to see what is ahead, but when going down, you cannot always see what is beneath you or if there is a step at all. I'm not sure if it's what Dr King meant, but I do believe that the imagery for me serves as a lesson in faith beyond the fall. For me it is not about taking a blind step where there is not staircase. Instead it is knowing that if you take a step not knowing if there is a staircase, falling is possible, but falling is not failure nor is falling definite. Try both. Try and maybe you fall, but you can get up and try again. Try taking a step and maybe you will land on a firm foundation and are able to keep pursuing what is next.

A twenty-one-year-old Australian poet named Erin Hanson wrote in a poem, "There is freedom waiting for you, On the breezes of the sky, And you ask "What if I fall?" Oh but my darling, What if you fly?" These words help me better handle the words of Dr King. They speak to the fact that our perspective about what could happen often alters our action and effects what should happen. The other impressive insight about this poem is that it was written by a young 21-year-old that still has the innocence to not worry about skeptic thoughts of crashing. Instead, she encourages a shifting of perspective that all of us could use in our LEAP OF FAITH.

Finally, Paul of Tarsus while writing a letter to a church in Corinth wrote, " That your faith should not stand in the wisdom of men, but in the power of God." (1 Corinthians 2:5) This scriptural quote constantly causes me to rest the hope of my faith in God. It is not in my own ability or lack thereof. Faith is not about what others will do or attempt to stop from happening. Our faith is in the power of an almighty, world-creating, all wise, very patience, well-networked, unmatched-in-love God who cares about us. With this fact, I encourage you to consider the same. Consider how great God is and how much He wants you to succeed even beyond your skill and the approval of others. Take the leap of faith! Faith is not easy, but it is necessary.

Most people can agree that faith is the main ingredient in pleasing God. Pleasing God and staying in relationship with God brings so many benefits and can bless many people. I remember while I was playing basketball at James Madison University. Our first official workout began on a track. The entire team walked confidently out onto the track surrounding the football field. The sun beamed on our brows, and the cool Harrisonburg breeze was just enough to make it a great day.

The coach handed each of my teammates and me a black duffel bag with purple handles. I opened it up with great childlike excitement expecting new basketball shoes, my practice jersey, and new shorts. To my surprise, I had been given running shoes. Track running shoes. Not high-top basketball shoes, but low-cut running shoes. I was as confused as a cat in a dog park. After lacing up the Nike Trailwinds, the coach then gave a speech. He started with, "Guys welcome to JMU Basketball. Today we run. Tomorrow we run. When the season begins, we run and in order to be at the top of the conference at the end of the season, you will still be running. Run around the track, up the bleachers, out of the stadium, and to the gym. You may cry, you may sweat, you may even throw up, but whatever you do, do not stop running." Wow?! I could not believe it. I had finally gained access to a lifelong dream to play Division 1 basketball, and the first work out did not even include a ball. One of the upper classmen leaned over to me and whispered, "Not what you were expecting huh, freshmeat." Freshmeat was the nickname for all freshmen on the squad. I did not answer I just looked at him. Then the coach spoke again with power. "I know you thought you were going to be shooting today, but if you cannot run your shooting will not matter." Running is the most important skill you will have this season. We cannot play basketball at this level without being able to run. That is not only true about running, it is also true about faith.

You cannot play basketball at that level without running, and similarly you cannot be the next level Christian that you know you are supposed to be without faith. I am not sure what you were expecting from this book but let me tell you the truth. The next 29 days are going to be like running around a track, up the bleachers, out of the sanctuary, and into a blessing. I lend you the same words that were given to me. You may cry, you may seat, you may even throw up, but whatever you do, do not stop. If you would commit to the following acts of faith for the next 29 days, it will be difficult for you not to grow in your faith.

—Dr. Dwight Shawrod Riddick II

directive to take a LEAP OF FAITH. It was through her prayer

Evangelize

The ABC Salvation Plan: Knowing the letters or characters of any given language is foundational to communicating effectively. Knowing the Plan of Salvation is foundational to a person receiving Jesus Christ as their Lord and Savior. The Jackson 5 sang "ABC, easy as one two three," so take a leap of faith today and move on down the road to share the ABC Plan of Salvation with someone.

A: Admit that you have sinned. **Romans 3:23** states, "For all have sinned, and come short of the glory of God;"

B: Believe that Jesus is God's Son, that He died for your sins, and that He rose from the dead. Believe that He ascended into heaven and that He is coming back again. "For God so loved the world, that he gave his only begotten Son, that whosoever believeth in him should not perish, but have everlasting life." **John 3:16**

C: Confess that Jesus is Lord. **John 1:12** declares, "Yet to all who did receive him, to those who believed in his name, he gave the right to become children of God—"

Write down what it was like when you received `Jesus Christ for yourself?

Day 2

Pray for Our Community

"Let us think of ways to motivate one another to acts of love and good works."

Hebrews 10:24

The song, "I Need You to Survive" is a very powerful song that speaks to community and being better together, both in the church and in our communities at large. Take a leap of faith today and listen to the song, meditate on it, and then pray for our churches and our political and community leaders to have and use godly wisdom; pray that all needs be supplied for everyone; pray that love is shown to one another, by words and actions, and most importantly; pray that we pray for each other and lift each other up.

Name 3 people in the community that you will pray for today?

Pray for Our Country

"I urge you, first of all, to pray for all people. Ask God to help them; intercede on their behalf, and give thanks for them. Pray this way for kings and all who are in authority so that we can live peaceful and quiet lives marked by godliness and dignity."

1 Timothy 2:1-2

Prayer is powerful and it works in numerous ways. Sometimes God will change things, situations, and even people according to His will. The apostle Matthew wrote, "May your Kingdom come soon. May your will be done on earth, as it is in heaven." (Matthew 6:10)

Sometimes He gives us the grace to accept and work through the situation we are in: "Each time he said, "My grace is all you need. My power works best in weakness." So now I am glad to boast about my weaknesses, so that the power of Christ can work through me." (2 Corinthians 12:9)

Other times He empowers us to overcome whatever is in our path: "I tell you the truth, you can say to this mountain, 'May you be lifted up and thrown into the sea,' and it will happen. But you must really believe it will happen and have no doubt in your heart." (Mark 11:23)

Any manner God answers, prayer works. Take a leap of faith today and pray for our president and our entire political system. Pray for our military members and their families. Pray for families everywhere. Pray for the homeless and pray for our climate.

Write out the Lord's Prayer.

Day 4

Pray for All Youth

"Children are a heritage from the LORD, offspring a reward from him."
Psalm 127:3 (NIV)

Most of us are familiar with the song lyrics, "Jesus loves the little children, all the children of the world . . . they are precious in His sight." This is evident in Matthew 19:13-15: "One day some parents brought their children to Jesus so he could lay his hands on them and pray for them. But the disciples scolded the parents for bothering him. But Jesus said, "Let the children come to me. Don't stop them! For the Kingdom of Heaven belongs to those who are like these children." And he placed his hands on their heads and blessed them before he left."

He loves them and is also protective of them: "But if you cause one of these little ones who trusts in me to fall into sin, it would be better for you to have a large millstone tied around your neck and be drowned in the depths of the sea." (Matthew 18:6)

From conception until death God has placed them in our care. As parents, grandparents, and family members, we have the privilege of praying and providing for our children. They are the future leaders of the church, our businesses, and our country. Today take a trip down memory lane and reflect over or look at pictures from your childhood, pictures of your children, grandchildren, and church and community pictures of youth you know. Then take a leap of faith and pray for our youth. Pray for wisdom on how to discipline and guide their lives. Pray for their salvation, education, and that the gifts God has placed in them be stirred up and they walk in the purpose and plan He has for them. Seek God's blessings over their family and their lives.

Name 3 students you will pray for today.

Day 5

Read John 17

"Study to shew thyself approved unto God, a workman that needeth not to be ashamed, rightly dividing the word of truth."
2 Timothy 2:15 (KJV)

The Gospel singer Dorothy Norwood wrote and sang the song, "Somebody Prayed for Me." The verse begins, "Somebody prayed for me, had me on their mind, they took the time and prayed for me. I'm so glad they prayed, I'm so glad they prayed, I'm so glad they prayed for me." How great is it to know that Jesus had you on His mind and took the time to pray for you because He wanted each one of us to be connected to the Father and each other through Him. (John 17:20-23)

Jesus wanted unity in His family. Because with unity there is peace and power. Today take a leap of faith and reflect on Jesus's prayer. Then ask yourself if you are reflecting the glory of Jesus in the church and in your community? Are you being humble in your actions and words? Are you showing hospitality? Are you living in harmony or causing discord? Are you living holy (set apart for God) or are you blending in with the world by your words, actions, and attitudes so much that no can tell that you belong to God? Remember, Jesus prayed for you to reflect His glory just as He had reflected His Father's glory.

Name 3 areas of life that you would like Jesus to pray to His Father about on your behalf.

_____

_____

_____

_____

_____

_____

_____

_____

_____

_____

_____

_____

_____

_____

_____

Day 6

Attend Bible Study

"Come close to God, and God will come close to you. Wash your hands, you sinners; purify your hearts, for your loyalty is divided between God and the world."
James 4:8

How do I draw closer to God? How do I get cleansed from my sins? How can I stop being tossed and turned between God's ways and the world's ways? We cannot become like Christ if we don't know Him. Jesus is revealed in the scriptures. But the Bible is not just a book *about* God. It is alive and is used to guide us, convict us, and transform our thinking. Take a leap of faith today and attend Bible study either in church or online because God's word will set you on the right path. "All Scripture is inspired by God and is useful to teach us what is true and to make us realize what is wrong in our lives. It corrects us when we are wrong and teaches us to do what is right." (2 Timothy 3:16)

Come back and write 1 take away or "aha" moment that you learned from Bible study today?

_____

_____

_____

_____

_____

_____

_____

_____

_____

_____

_____

_____

_____

_____

_____

_____

_____

_____

Invite Someone to Church Part 1

"And let us consider how we may spur one another on toward love and good deeds, not giving up meeting together, as some are in the habit of doing, but encouraging one another—and all the more as you see the Day approaching."
Hebrews 10:25

Over the years there have been many false predictions of the world coming to an end and the extinction of humanity, yet we are still here. Only God knows the day or the hour when Jesus will return. So we shouldn't agonize or walk in fear about when He's coming back, but our goal should be ensuring that we are living in a way that is pleasing to Him. People are dealing with many challenges and need hope and encouragement. Many are burdened about how they will make it to the next minute, day, or moment. Take a leap of faith and invite someone you know who needs encouragement to go to church with you and then go the extra mile and treat them to lunch afterwards for fellowship.

List 3 people that you are going to invite to church.

Invite Someone to Church Part 2

"Therefore go and make disciples of all nations, baptizing them in the name of the Father and of the Son and of the Holy Spirit."
Matthew 28:19

Matthew 28:19 is a command from Jesus not a request. In our families, on our jobs, and in our communities, there are people we know who need Jesus, but we do not extend the invitation to come to church. We don't have any discussions in order to share the plan of salvation with anyone. We keep Jesus to ourselves instead of proclaiming the good news to all people. But He said go make disciples. This may involve crossing physical, cultural, and even spiritual barriers. So, take a leap of faith today and invite someone who you know is not saved to come to church. Invite them over or take them out afterwards to discuss the service and the sermon that was preached.

Name 2 places you can go to find someone to invite to church.

_____
_____
_____
_____
_____
_____
_____
_____
_____
_____
_____
_____
_____
_____
_____

Abstain from TV

> "So we fix our eyes not on what is seen, but on what is unseen, since what is seen is temporary, but what is unseen is eternal."
> **2 Corinthians 4:18**

A 2015 study by the Harvard School of Public Health found that viewing more than two hours of TV daily was linked to an increased risk of type 2 diabetes and heart disease, and more than three hours of daily viewing increased the risk of premature death. The U.S. News & World Report also found that that it can damage your relationships, cause delayed verbal skills in children, increase aggression, and rob us of sleep and rest.

In a letter to the Corinthian church, the apostle Paul encourages us to fix our attention on what is unseen—things of the Spirit that are eternal—as opposed to things that are seen—things that are worldly and temporary. Allow today to be a rest from your favorite shows on television, whether it be news, sports, reality TV, or dramatic shows and films. Spend time gazing on things which are unseen.

Switch your focus and name 2 attributes of God that you value the most? (Example: God's power, healing, majesty, provision, glory, etc.)

Day 10

Abstain from Social Media

But seek first his kingdom and his righteousness, and all these things will be given to you as well.
Matthew 6:33

Facebook, Twitter, Instagram and Snapchat (to name a few) are popular social media networks which are designed and created to connect and bring people together. The rise of social media has made us more connected than we have ever been. For some, social media is the first thing checked in the morning and the last thing checked before falling asleep. But just as television has been found to disturb rest and possibly damage your relationships, too much time on social media leads to unhappiness, isolation, and low-self esteem as we try to create the perfect post for that elusive "like."

For many of us, we will log into Facebook before looking at a "Faith Book;" send out a "tweet" to our friends before sending up a "thank you" to our heavenly Father; start a chat without first chatting with our Savior. Social Media can be a positive tool of connection and communication. Perhaps God would appreciate our first connection be made with Him before everyone else with the world. Take a day to seek God first and take a break from social media.

Write a short prayer to God. Whatever you would say, just write it down. Let today's journal become your spiritual social media.

A Well-being Call

"Love your neighbor as yourself."
Matthew 22:39

In his 1970s hit "Lean on Me" Bill Withers writes, "Sometimes in our lives we all have pain, we all have sorrow…" In those moments when we were suffering pain, going through a moment of sorrow, or even on a day in which everything may be going well, isn't it good to have someone pick up the phone and call and check up on you without asking for anything? Or maybe you can remember the time where you felt you couldn't go on, was dealing with a chronic illness, or life just seemed to come at you from every side, and no one reached out. The truth is that many of us love it when someone reaches out to us, but when was the last time you reached out to someone else. Jesus teaches that one of the greatest commandments is to love your neighbor as yourself. So today, show love for a neighbor or that person that keeps crossing your mind and call them just to check on them.

Name 2 people that you could call today.

Day 12

Reconcile an Estranged Relationship

"Bear with each other and forgive one another if any of you has a grievance against someone. Forgive as the Lord forgave you."
Colossians 3:13

How long has it been since you talked to that sibling, relative, friend, or that loved one? If we would be honest, it has been quite some time. It may have been so long that you may not remember why you stopped speaking or what was the source of the conflict. Allow me to encourage you to reach out to that one who you haven't heard from or spoken to in a while. Lay aside your pride. You may need to forgive them, and perhaps, they may need to forgive you. We may not have as much time as we think we have to reconcile with those who have become estranged. There is a peace and a liberty that comes with forgiving others.

Why do you think reconciling an estranged relationship is important?

_____
_____
_____
_____
_____
_____
_____
_____
_____
_____
_____
_____
_____
_____
_____
_____
_____

Day 13

Make a Gratitude List

"In everything give thanks; for this is the will of God in Christ Jesus for you."
1 Thessalonians. 5:18

One of my favorite hymns of the church is penned by a nineteenth century hymn writer by the name of Johnson Oatman, Jr. He writes,

> "When upon life's billows you are tempest-tossed/When you are discouraged, thinking all is lost/Count your many blessings; name them one by one/And it will surprise you what the Lord has done."

True words indeed! But we often rush through life. We miss opportunities because we don't take the time to slow down or stop. Whenever you get to a place where it seems as if life is swallowing you whole, take a moment to consider what the Lord has already done for you. Literally, take out a legal pad, a journal, or open the Notes app in your mobile device, and make a list of the blessings the Lord has bestowed upon you. A gratitude list not only makes you feel more positive about life but it equips you to better handle life's adversities.

List 10 things that you are grateful for.

Make or Buy a Gift

"Do to others as you would have them do to you."
Luke 6:31

The old adage states, "What you make happen for others God will make happen for you." Perhaps, the blessing you stand in need of is already in your hands. That's just it. When you release what is in your hands into someone else's hands, God sees your benevolence as an opportunity to bless you again. Find it in your heart to make someone's day with the gift that is in your hands. Galatians 6:7 (KJV) says, "Be not deceived; God is not mocked: for whatsoever a man soweth, that shall he also reap." What we do for others are the seeds we sow that will produce a harvest for us.

List 3 people that you could make or buy a gift for. Then choose one of the three and do it.

Day 15

Buy or Make Lunch for Someone

"Anyone who has two shirts should share with the one who has none, and anyone who has food should do the same."
Luke 3:11

Eating can be defined as the consumption of food and liquid to sustain life and to meet our body's basic needs for growth, development, and function. Every cell in the body depends on a continuous supply of calories and nutrients obtained through food. Eating and food, however, also have symbolic meanings associated with love, sensuality, comfort, stress reduction, security, reward, and power. It is likely you will have a meal today. It is also likely that you know someone that will have a meal today. The idea of today's leap of faith is that you make or purchase a meal for someone. Isaiah 58:10 says, "Feed the hungry, and help those in trouble. Then your light will shine out from the darkness, and the darkness around you will be as bright as noon."

List 2 people that you could buy or make lunch for and write what type of lunch you plan to provide.

Day 16

Evangelize Day 2

The **4 Spiritual Laws Plan of Salvation:** Sharing the good news and offering the plan of salvation is as easy as one, two, three, four. Sharing the good news is the catalyst to a heart change in those around you. Romans 10:14 (KJV) says, "How, then, can they call on him they have not believed in? And how can they preach unless they are sent? As it is written: How beautiful are the feet of those who bring good news."

If you don't already know these scriptures, write them out on note cards and practice them. Then take a leap of faith and share this plan of salvation with someone God has put on your heart.

John 3:16— "For God so loved the world that he gave his one and only Son, that whoever believes in him shall not perish but have eternal life."

Romans 3:23— "for all have sinned and fall short of the glory of God,"

Romans 5:8— "But God demonstrates his own love for us in this: While we were still sinners, Christ died for us."

John 1:12— "Yet to all who did receive him, to those who believed in his name, he gave the right to become children of God—"

Read these 4 Spiritual laws 20 times today at then write which 2 people you will share it with:

The laws are:
1) God loves you and has a plan for your life.
2) Man is sinful and sin separates us from God so we cannot experience the fullness of His love.

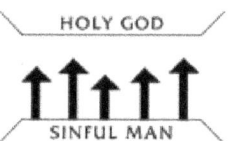

3) Jesus is God's only provision to remove sin. Jesus bridges the gap between God and humanity.

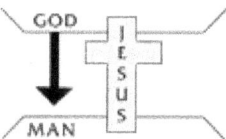

4) You must receive Jesus personally and then be freed from sin and experience God's love.

Pray the payer of salvation:
Dear Lord Jesus,
Thank You for dying on the cross for my sin. Please forgive me. Come into my life. I receive You as my Lord and Savior. Now, help me to live for You the rest of this life.
In the name of Jesus I pray,
Amen.

_____

_____

_____

_____

_____

_____

Give 3-5 Genuine Compliments

"Pleasant words are like a honeycomb; sweetness to the soul and health to the bones."
Proverbs 16:24

Giving a genuine compliment is an amazing positivity boost! But compliments are not only good for the recipients—they're good for the people who give them as well. When you go out of your way to say something nice and give thoughtful praise to another person, it amplifies your self-confidence and nourishes your self-esteem.

Be a source of positivity and happiness in the lives of others. Everything you give will come back to you many times over. Take a few moments to think about the last time someone gave you a genuine compliment—and not just a casual compliment, but a genuine piece of specific, thoughtful praise. How did it make you feel?

Make it your business to genuinely make someone's day by sharing a compliment from the heart.

Write 5 compliments that you would like to hear from someone? Then go share 5 compliments with someone else.

Day 18

Volunteer at a School

"God has given each of you a gift from his great variety of spiritual gifts. Use them well to serve one another."
1 Peter 4:10

There are a great number of things that we as Christ followers can "find our hands to do." One of which is to volunteer your time. With busy lives, it can be hard to find time to volunteer. However, the benefits of volunteering can be enormous. Volunteering offers vital help to people in need, worthwhile causes, and the community, but the benefits can be even greater for you, the volunteer.

In our schools there is a great need for willing, loving, and able-bodied people to lend a helping hand. Taking things off the plate of teachers, administration, and staff frees them up to do what they do best, which is to educate our children.

So, which school will you volunteer at today?

Name 1 school that you could visit today.

_____
_____
_____
_____
_____
_____
_____
_____
_____
_____
_____
_____
_____
_____
_____
_____
_____

Day 19

Donate Used Goods to Goodwill

"And don't forget to do good and to share with those in need. These are the sacrifices that please God."
Hebrews 13:16

When it comes time to clean out those closets, drawers, attics, and cabinets, Goodwill is a convenient choice for dropping off those items you want to donate. As much as you may want to hold on to that suit, dress, or shoes, I am certain that they will be a blessing to someone else. And, more importantly, when you share with those in need, it pleases God! It's in these moments that we become the hands and feet of God.

Write down the address of the nearest Goodwill, Salvation Army, or other location that could receive your donation.

Day 20

30-Minute Physical Activity

"For bodily exercise profiteth little: but godliness is profitable unto all things, having promise of the life that now is, and of that which is to come."
1Titus 4:8

The apostle would have Timothy to instill into the minds of Christians such sentiments as might prevent their being seduced by the Judaizing teachers. The Jewish traditions, which some people fill their heads with, have nothing to do with them. However, **exercise** thyself rather unto godliness; that is, mind practical religion. Those who would be godly must **exercise** themselves unto godliness; it requires a constant **exercise**. The reason is taken from the fain of godliness; bodily **exercise** profits little, or for a little time. There is a great deal to be got by godliness; it will be of use to us in the whole of our life, for it has the promise of the life that now is, and of that which is to come. The gain of godliness lies much in the promise: and the promises made to godly people relate to the life that now is, but especially they relate to the life that is to come. Under the Old Testament, the promises were mostly of temporal blessings, but under the New Testament of spiritual and eternal blessings. If godly people have but little of the good things of the life that now is, yet it shall be made up to them in the good things of the life that is to come.

What exercise are you going to do today?

Day 21

Spend Time in a Garden or in Nature

"And the LORD God took the man, and put him into the garden of Eden to dress it and to keep it."
Genesis 2:15

This chapter is an appendix to the history of the creation, more particularly explaining and enlarging upon that part of the history that relates immediately to man, the favorite of this lower world. The place appointed for Adam's residence was a garden; not an ivory house nor a palace overlaid with gold, but a garden, furnished and adorned by nature, not by art.

Man was made out of paradise, for after God had formed him, He put him into the garden; he was made of common clay, not of paradise-dust. He lived out of Eden before he lived in it, that he might see that all the comforts of his paradise-state were owing to God's free grace. He could not plead a tenant-right to the garden, for he was not born upon the premises, nor had anything but what he received; all boasting was hereby forever excluded.

John19:41 states, "Now in the place where he was crucified there was a garden; and in the garden a new sepulchre, wherein was never man yet laid."

Come back and write down what you observed or what stood out the most to you during your garden experience.

_____

_____

_____

_____

_____

_____

_____

_____

_____

_____

_____

_____

_____

_____

_____

_____

_____

_____

Day 22

Study a Member of the "Hebrews Hall of Faith"

For their record-breaking statistics, exceptional accolades and, incredible athletic ability, Gale Sayers, "Mean" Joe Greene, Jerry Rice, Emmitt Smith, and Ray Lewis are all members of the Pro Football Hall of Fame. These players displayed grit, hard work, and determination throughout the course of their storied careers. They have been a part of championship-winning teams, and they have garnered individual awards for their productivity while competing in the National Football League. Their place in the Pro Football Hall of Fame immortalizes them forever.

There is another "Hall" found in the eleventh chapter of Hebrews. This Hall consists of persons whose faith made them famous: Abel, Enoch, Sarah, Gideon, Samuel, and Rahab. These were men and women who were the epitome of what faith is and line the Hall of Faith with stories of deliverance and obedience to Almighty God

Read Hebrews 11 today and select some of the names listed in the Hall of Faith. Study their story and allow God to speak to you through what He did in their lives.

After reading Hebrews 11, which of the Hall of Faith members stood out to you the most and why?

Visit the Library

"Do not throw away your confidence, which has a great reward."
Hebrews 10:38

Reading is fundamental is a popular phrase in the United States often used to explain how simple things could be if we just read. Have you ever tried to assemble a desk or bookshelf without reading the instructions? Or maybe you've tried a new recipe but failed to use the correct measurements and it just didn't turn out like you expected. Reading not only helps guide us to a wanted destination, it also provides us with the tools necessary to gain more knowledge. Reading can help reduce stress, expand vocabulary, as well as increase focus, concentration, and memory for people of all ages.

Studies have also shown that reading doesn't just improve your knowledge, it can help fight depression, improve confidence, and aid in making better decisions. Visiting the library and diving into a good book can give you a refreshed perspective of your own life with renewed understanding.

Write the name of the librarian or the name of a book that you SAW (don't have to read it all) that piqued your interest.

Day 24

Six Steps of Success

When those who were carrying the ark of the LORD had taken six steps, he sacrificed a bull and a fattened calf.
2 Samuel 6:13

Once King David finally realized that God's presence was more important than any reason he could ever have for being mad at God, he went and reacquired the Ark of the Covenant. In recognition of what God had done, they stopped and sacrificed an offering every six steps! First of all, that is a lot of fattened calf! Secondly, it took intentional commitment and patience.

Today let's take Six Steps of Success:

Step 1: 1:00 PM – Read the 23 Psalm

Step 2: 2:00 PM – Pause and whisper the Lord's Prayer aloud (found in Matthew 6:9-13)

Step 3: 3:00 PM – Read the 10 Commandments (found in Exodus 20:1-17)

Step 4: 4:00 PM – Write 4 things you are thankful for.

Step 5: 5:00 PM – Whisper a prayer of repentance (Lord I am sorry for _____)

Step 6: 6:00 PM – Say Hallelujah 3 times loud enough for you to hear it.

A plan can take you a long way, and the steps of a good man have been ordered and are often blessed by the Lord.

From the 6 steps you took today, which step made the greatest impact and why?

_____
_____
_____
_____
_____
_____
_____
_____
_____
_____
_____
_____
_____
_____
_____
_____
_____
_____

Day 25

Learn A New Vocabulary Word

After the victory, the Lord instructed Moses, "Write this down on a scroll as a permanent reminder, and read it aloud to Joshua. I will erase the memory of Amalek from under heaven,"
Exodus 17:13

In 3rd Century BC, Greek mathematician and inventor Archimedes was supervising the construction of the largest ship ever. While contemplating how to make a vessel of that magnitude float, suddenly, "Eureka!" He created the law of buoyancy, which is still referred to today as Archimedes Law.

Archimedes would have never created the law of buoyancy had he not tried something new. Learning is a lifelong experience that gives us the opportunity to navigate, innovate, and create. Learning a new vocabulary word today will increase your knowledge, but more importantly will help to mold and catapult the generations that will come after you.

What is your newly-learned word for the day? What does it mean and write it down using it in a sentence?

Day 26

Write A Prayer

> Then the LORD replied: "Write down the revelation and make it plain on tablets so that a herald may run with it.
> **Habakkuk 2:2**

Today on a sheet of paper (not digital) write out your prayer. Include in your prayer:

*A*doration – Statements of worship about who God is. Adore him in your prayer.

*C*onfession – Include a sentence or two naming a specific sin, mistake, or habit that you know you have committed that God may not be pleased with.

*T*hanksgiving – Identify five things in your prayer that you are grateful for, that you know God has done for you.

*S*upplication – Ask God for something. In this prayer just pick one thing and then start believing.

After you have written this prayer, place it in an envelope. Seal it. Write on the Envelope, "I BELIEVE GOD" and include the date. Then either pin the envelope to a wall somewhere you can see it. Whenever God answers this prayer, whether it's within days, weeks, months, or years, open the envelope, share the answered prayer with someone, and repeat this "write a prayer" faith exercise. Sometimes God shows you want you say to Him. So, say it loud and proud and then watch God and His marvelous ACTS bless you.

Since you are writing your prayer on a separate sheet of paper to place in an envelope, please share here what it felt like to write your prayer down. Be honest:

Recommended readings of books filled with written prayers that Pastor Riddick has enjoyed are:

Copeland, German. **Prayers that Avail Much 25th Anniversary Edition**.
  Harrison House, 2005

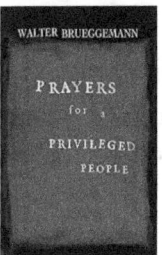

Brueggemann, Walter. **Prayers of a Privileged People**.
  Abingdon Press 2008

Mason-Underdue, Lucretia. **Real Prayers for Real People**.
  Final Step Publishing 2019

Groeschel, Craig. **Dangerous Prayers: Because Following Jesus Was Never Meant To Be Safe**.
  Zondervan Publishing 2020

Day 27

Parking Lot Prayer

"Now Jabez was more honorable than his brothers, and his mother called his name Jabez, saying, 'Because I bore him in pain.' And Jabez called on the God of Israel saying, 'Oh, that You would bless me indeed, and enlarge my territory, that Your hand would be with me, and that You would keep me from evil, that I may not cause pain.' So God granted him what he requested."
1 Chronicles 4:10

Today, take five minutes and pull into the parking lot of a church, non-profit organization, or a business and pray. It can be yours or a random place; the goal is simply to pray that God do for them what he did for Jabez.

Jabez was a peculiar member of his family that prayed a peculiar prayer. You will find that when you are different than others you are expected to believe God for the unique. If you can think and pray it, God can do it. Today bless someone with a prayer for expansion.

What parking lots are near you or on your morning route that you could pull into today for prayer?

In God We Trust

Some trust in chariots and some in horses, but we trust in the name of the LORD our God.
Psalm 20:7

Today, let's encourage someone to trust God. Place $1 (you may do more if you'd like) in an envelope with a scripture or handwritten note. Highlight or circle on the bill the words, "IN GOD WE TRUST." Hand this to a random person that you do not know and keep walking. The goal is to remind them that they should trust God, while simultaneously you will be TRUSTING that GOD has led you to the right person.

Trusting God is the first step to receiving all He has for you and becoming all He wants you to be in order to serve others.

What scripture about trusting God are you going to write on the envelope today?

Day 29

Evangelize Day 3

The **Romans Road Plan of Salvation**: During the time of the Roman Empire it was said that all roads lead to Rome and they literally did. Rome was built right in the center of the Empire and the stone roads that were made throughout all the Roman Provinces led people to Rome. This road system helped make the Roman Empire very strong. The Romans Road Plan of Salvation is similar in that it uses several different scriptures (roads) throughout the book of Romans to lead people to Jesus Christ, who was strong enough to overcome death and save us from our sins. Take a leap of faith today and lead someone down the Romans Road Plan of Salvation to receive Jesus as their personal Savior.

Romans 3:23— "for all have sinned and fall short of the glory of God,"

Romans 5:8— "But God demonstrates his own love for us in this: While we were still sinners, Christ died for us."

Romans 6:23— "For the wages of sin is death, but the gift of God is eternal life in Christ Jesus our Lord."

Romans 10:9-10— "If you declare with your mouth, "Jesus is Lord," and believe in your heart that God raised him from the dead, you will be saved. For it is with your heart that you believe and are justified, and it is with your mouth that you profess your faith and are saved."

Romans 10:13— for, "Everyone who calls on the name of the Lord will be saved."

Why is salvation important to you?

www.ingramcontent.com/pod-product-compliance
Lightning Source LLC
Chambersburg PA
CBHW071032080526
44587CB00015B/2580